Praise for John Sweet:

John has been a mainstay small press poet for as long as I can remember his voice ringing out, prevalent and relevant, exposing contemporary political, social, economic and personal issues for what they truly are.

John's style is vivid, clear and edgy, pulling no punches, telling it like it is, reminding us that certain actions, behaviors, and ideologies are never acceptable and that we need to be better than we are if we expect to survive beyond today with any modicum of fair-play, decency, honor, and self-respect. He expresses what needs to be expressed.

This special book contains many of John's best poems, vivid, sculpted perfectly, precisely, leaping off the pages, no ambiguity or agnosticism, no equivocation here. John is not only a poet but also a prophet. I am always enlightened and engaged, sometimes amused and amazed when I read his poems. You will be too. There is no mistaking it: John Sweet is the real deal.

- Michael Estabrook, *The Poet's Curse: A Miscellany*

A Dead Man, Either Way

Poems by John Sweet

Kung Fu Treachery Press
Rancho Cucamonga, CA

Copyright © John Sweet, 2020
First Edition 1 3 5 7 9 10 8 6 4 2
ISBN: 978-1-952411-01-4
LCCN: 2020934722

Cover image: John Sweet
Title page image: Jon Lee Grafton
Author photo: John Sweet
All rights reserved. No part of this publication may be reproduced or transmitted in any form or by any means, electronic or mechanical, including photocopying, recording or by info retrieval system, without prior written permission from the author.

With thanks to the editors at *Ascent Aspirations, Asphodel Madness, Burning Word, Clockhouse, Dead Snakes, Easy Street, Eclectica, Full of Crow, Half-Drunk Muse, Identity Theory, Juxtaprose, Midnight Lane Boutique, Moria, Mortal Corkscrew, My Favorite Bullet, Nerve Cowboy, Pyrokinection, Rasputin, Ten Pages Press, Tin Lustre Mobile, Tryst, Underground Voices, Winamop, Yellow Mama* and *Ygdrasil*, where many of these poems previously appeared, sometimes in slightly different forms.

TABLE OF CONTENTS

selected poems (2005-2016)

the burning flag / 1

permafrost / 4

the myth, reconsidered / 5

some facts / 7

the hours, pressing down / 8

explaining the bleeding horse / 9

like sugar for the blood / 11

the way it happens / 13

EVERY 14 SECONDS AIDS TURNS A CHILD INTO AN ORPHAN / 15

plane falling from 30,000 feet / 16

gunman kills seven, himself / 18

landscape, without apology / 22

where the sounds go when they escape our throats / 24

in a room, blindly / 26

marie / 27

indigenous poem / 28

in the dream of ordinary shame / 30

the sun is god's face bleeding down / 31

cage / 33

the sun, the clouds, the bottomless sky / 36

manifest destiny: a literal translation / 37

gira / 38

the face of god, burned / 40

small moment of ascension in the desperate season / 40

the written word disguised as truth / 43

opened her arms, said come home / 45

the necessity of pain and fear / 46

the poem is only a means of killing time / 47

hangman / 49

the forest's edge and what we found there / 50

poem in the shadow of the bleeding horse / 52

far away / 53

meditation on futility / 54

a priest with his hands cut off standing in the
    shallow light of god / 55

church on fire / 58

upstate landscape w/ minor premonition / 60

: : / 61

imaginary poem while waiting for rain / 62

the dominion of light, loosely translated / 66

the world, awake / 67

words like black blood from the frozen ground: a psalm / 68

man drowning in a second story room / 70

holy poem, after the death of god / 72

not the dream, but everything that comes after / 73

the blood factory, revisited / 75

burying the sun / 76

the girl on fire tells you what she knows about love / 78

room filled with broken objects / 79

a pale yellow sun in a plain white house / 81

the poet runs out of words / 83

number 29, 1950, second attempt / 85

to starve in a house we call home / 86

a footnote to the season of rust / 88

stealing the title to atwood's notes towards a poem
    that can never be written / 90

the body dissected, the cancer laid bare (later) / 92

the collapse of the human cathedral: a premonition / 95

building something darker in the ruins
    of the human cathedral / 97

a cold spring afternoon in the world of darker truths / 99

blue / 101

indian summer / 103

shaped by fire / 104

in the afternoon of bitter confessions / 105

desperate poem from the season of rust / 107

myself a bastard son / 108

letter to kurt cobain, seven years dead,
    on his 35th birthday / 110

the moment with clarity, but no definition / 111

faith in nothing: a confession / 112

black chalk / 114

sparrow / 116

we are nothing and nothing can save us / 118

bird imagery 2 / 120

broken hand w/ mirror / 121

blue skied surrender / 122

postcard to california / 124

splendour / 125

into view / 126

one for j / 127

ash wilderness / 128

a forest / 129

the village, on fire / 130

notes on finding religion / 132

the sick child in a room filled w/grey light / 133

leonard sends news of another dead poet / 134

max ernst, all is forgiven / 135

the indifferent heart / 136

no luck, only slowly dying machines / 138

the sky, blatantly / 139

painting a poem for ernst, who was never my father / 140

an accumulation of ghosts / 142

his later years / 143

poem while watching dali paint the iridescent sky / 144

what i said to gorky / 145

poem for a year of election / 147

icarus, one last time / 148

with tired eyes / 150

why every poem should be the last one / 151

without a name, without armor / 153

inwards / 154

man crawling on the ocean floor / 156

lullaby, for beth / 158

the ascension / 160

each dog needs a name / 162

boy found dead in the river's veins / 163

carver's bones / 165

entropy / 167

first poem from the season of fear / 169

no blood no feathers / 171

poet as crow/as starving dog/as himself / 172

driving back from the coast / 174

pyrrh / 175

tora / 176

after the age of enlightenment / 177

all hope edged w/ frost / 178

a gift, belated / 179

unfinished film about prison / 180

the well of knowledge / 181

on the occasion of my four year-old son
    learning how to draw a peace sign / 182

blood in the spaces between what we say
    and what we mean / 184

halcyon / 187

things that can burn / 188

golgotha, which is always within / 189

in the joy of small truths / 190

desire / 191

shiva's blues / 192

first portrait of st maria in the style of dali / 193

a room of truths, a house of rage / 195

easter / 196

not the end of everything, but still / 198

new poems - recent past and unforeseeable future

and everything lost, and nothing ever found / 201

a new testament / 203

in the aftermath of the assassination
   of the false king / 204

against empire / 209

incantation for the refused / 210

but who among us sings and who forgets
   the reasons why? / 213

distant king / 220

typhon's blues / 222

a series of idle threats / 223

mantra for beaten dogs / 226

final poem from a blue notebook / 228

speech in the ruins of what was given to me / 232

traitor / 233

*Every second that you cling to life,
you have to feel alive*

- Mark Burgess

selected poems
2005 - 2016

the burning flag

tired of the sound of my voice
in these mostly empty rooms and
tired of the silence that follows

tired of this woman who
calls me a monster

who stands in the cold april rain
outside my house
with the bones of her dead children
piled at her feet

blames me for
what's gone wrong in her life
and i'm sorry for the pain of others
but i feel no guilt

i believe in jesus christ
but not his miracles

listen

we kill what we fear

we force our convictions down

the throats of those we hate

do you believe in democracy?

did you spend the
second world war in a cage in
california because of the
color of your skin?

all your leaders have ever
wanted to protect themselves from
is you

all the priests have ever wanted
are your children

and were you taught that
murder is wrong?

do you understand why
andrea yates is still alive?

and when i finally open my door
the woman is gone
but there is a
young boy lying in the street

there is the car that hit him
and the man who drove it

the sound of
an ambulance approaching

this thought that
none of us are ever really saved

permafrost

was suddenly mortal in the
cold blue sunlight of my 35th winter

was lost in a room w/ a stranger and
her sister and both of them naked
and one of them crying and we
were far beyond the point where
words would help explain anything

i was considering rothko,
wrists slashed and overdosed on
his kitchen floor

i was considering his daughter

the ease with which pain
spreads out from the core

the myth, reconsidered

your words are not visions from god
and mine are only bad jokes
and this is where we stand

beauty caught in the tar of remorse
and that money is blood

that your pills are all dull knives
and every priest a rapist

ask your sons

step into the vague blue light of
any october afternoon
and consider how many days you've
wasted waiting to be forgiven

consider how many miles you drove
to reach the burning house

your father drunk
or maybe only dead
and whatever the last thing he
said to you was

the ticking of his watch as he
lay dying in a hospital bed

the first plane without warning
tearing the north tower
wide open

some facts

the bird says nothing,
but its throat fills w/ blood

the old man is blind

sits in his house long after
it's burned down to
ash and memory

writes poems about the
women he's loved
but then misplaces them
and the spaces between gods
are just lies w/ pretty
names

the phone ringing at 2 a.m.
is a profound threat

someone has died
whether you answer it or
                    not

the hours, pressing down

she says it's okay
but then starts to bleed

says there are prayers
that will stop it
and she says she knows a man

just has to get home
before her boyfriend

just needs some money

says nothing
but gets dressed and leaves
in the first blueblack
light of morning

disappears
for fifteen years

explaining the bleeding horse

man says
but this is just the
same poem written over and over

says america is more than
palaces of gold built on
the bones of indians

stops to take a drink and then
the door is kicked open

the cop shot dead

twenty miles south of
the town i grew up in with the
smell of meth and the
taste of ashes

the crosses on fire
and what i tell him is that
beauty needs ugliness to define it

let the dogs go too long
without food
and they'll eat your children

drag your enemy through
the streets of whatever place
you call home and he will
eventually be reduced to
memory and pale white light

show him mercy and
he'll rape your daughter

she'll tell you she
loves him

a truth that will bring
your house
crashing down around you

like sugar for the blood

cold yellow light on a sunday afternoon
and i apologize for nothing

i have no use for
burroughs or bukowski

edie is dead
and andrea
and all of your patron saints are
nowhere to be found

none of your cities
were ever meant to last forever

and i am tired of being hungry and i am
tired of being lost
but all of these houses look the same

all of these roads end without warning
at cemeteries or abandoned factories or
rivers with indian names in this land
where there are no indians and the
girl didn't jump she fell

four stories and drunk and left her
three year old daughter with nothing

but a missing father

the pacific was only a dream

3000 light years away and
when i stand in the shadow of this bridge
i have nothing of my own

when i pick up my son he cries

we are always on
the verge of being lost

the way it happens

this man on the bridge
falling or jumping
or holding a rock with both hands

dropping it
and the windshield of the car below
parting like violent water

the woman's face split in two
and your sister on the phone
saying she's pregnant

blood pooling on the floor where
you've left the idea of a mother
murdering her son with a butcher knife

the sky where it
pours itself over the landscape

the rock as it falls and the woman
as she turns to her husband and smiles

the pair of hands attached to a
person that no one knows

these fifteen crosses planted in
the ground in colorado
and the fact that nothing grows

your sister on the phone
saying she lost the baby

saying the blood
won't come off her hands
and the fact that nothing falls
out of the sky

the way she describes
the fetus to you

the idea that
none of these wars can ever
really be won

the man on the bridge jumping
and then falling
and then breaking through the ice

his apartment
and all of the places
a note was never left

all of the people it was
never addressed to

the body not found until spring

EVERY 14 SECONDS AIDS TURNS A CHILD INTO AN ORPHAN

or this 13 year-old kid next door who
stands in his front yard
waving a gun while
i move the baby away from the window

this idea that democracy doesn't mean
the same thing for the rich as
it does for the poor

or maybe no ideas at all

maybe just a silent prayer for
jessica lunsford which
tastes like nothing more than the shit
that spills from the mouths
of politicians

maybe just a prayer for myself

a blessing for a my children or a
promise to my wife or a story that
begins this 13 year-old kid next door
who stands in his front yard
waving a gun

a story that ends
without someone dying

it happens from time to time

plane falling from 30,000 feet

it's only a small field
in another state

it's only the bodies of
the two young girls found there

my children asleep and a
storm moving in and the woman
next door standing on the sidewalk and
screaming into a phone

says no one fucks with her kids

says NO ONE FUCKS WITH HER KIDS
like maybe the war is over

like maybe we've won

all the dead soldiers in their
indifferent graves and all of the
sons and daughters they raped thrown
into a pile at the edge of town

set on fire maybe or maybe left
for the dogs and it's only
a rock dropped from a freeway bridge

it's only the face of the bride
split in two

her past left facing her future
but seeing nothing

seeing the sky through the eyes of
two young girls found
dead in a field

impossible and blue and
neverending

gunman kills seven, himself

and what the indians want
is their land back

what the days taste like is dirt

a waitress in the bathroom
snorting crank on one on the floor
with her wrists slashed

and both of them live and
who they hate is themselves and what they
find are men who will love them
                            for this

and do the stories even matter if you
know how they'll end?

is a dying sun as important
as the bank
foreclosing on your house?

listen

all i've ever written about is myself

no one deserves to die on

their knees but it happens

look at lorca

look past him

all of these lives ruled by pain and fear

these trailers at the edge of town

at the edge of the highway

your boyfriend in a bedroom here
with someone else's wife

a hundred christs
nailed to a hundred crosses

beautiful in
the cold grey light of march
and then meaningless

landscape, without apology

and this is not my home
but i'm
unable to shake it

dead trees rising up
out of black water and
the sounds of trains always
moving away

a sky so blue and empty
it leaves no place for
any god to hide
and there is a woman
three thousand miles away who
insists i cannot write about
things i don't understand

there is the man she loves
between us

we make an uncertain triangle
and she is
sometimes distracted by
the sound of the ocean and
i am constantly afraid of
hearing my son cry out
in pain

he's too small to know
anything but
unconditional love and too
beautiful to remain
unscarred

he is always on
the edge of whatever
landscape i'm describing

i need this to be a
hopeful thing

where the sounds go when they escape our throats

my gift to you
is the rapid fluttering
of wings

you hold it briefly
then let it go
and i was young when
gorky locked the door and
secured the rope

younger still when
lennon's blood
was washed away

and i've become a man
who hates his job

have become
a son without a father

we have maps
you see
but no real idea where
we are

no idea where
the sounds go when they
escape our throats

we are whatever it is
that comes after
lost

in a room, blindly

Not lies, really,
but truths that can't be proven.

The ghosts of Aztecs,
of Incas.

Parking lots.

Palaces.

Man rolls the dice to see which of
the children will starve,
and then the bomb goes off.

Seventeen dead, blood everywhere,
the pews of the church on fire.

The runoff from the mill
dumped into the river.

Close your eyes and picture it.

The first time we met and then,
two years later,
the first time we made love.

Oceans on every side of us,
wars to the south,
to the east,
and I told you you were beautiful.

Had no words beyond that,
only abstractions.

Only need.

Thirty seven years old and
suddenly no longer blind and,
in the mountains,
the killers were making new plans.

In town,
the streetlights were coming on.

It seemed almost possible
we would find our way home.

marie

never
regretted
drinking yr
blood
but i'm sorry i
confused yr
smile w/ prayer

i'm sorry for
yr sister's
crucifixion

for the baby
waiting to be
found in an
empty apartment

kept calling
my name, but
i was already
gone

indigenous poem

this place that we call
the age of beliefs

these days that push and pull

that bleed into one another
until all i can remember is the
silent glare of sunlight on chrome

the shadows of trees as they
stutter across the windshield

not lost
but never quite anywhere
and then the simple fact of
this poet found dead behind the
wheel of a borrowed car

these streets that begin to
resemble de chirico's

doors locked against our arrival
and children locked in cages

their tentative smiles
or their useless screams

the smell of burning flesh
your faith in humanity

in the dream of ordinary shame

you should believe in
messiahs conceived by man

you should believe

there will be an end to poets

an end to words and to politicians
and we will be here in this empty house with
nothing between us but the corpses
of the disappeared

we will consider the moment where christ
clenches his hands into bleeding fists

the moment where the sun reaches
its highest point and the power fails and
the prisons are all filled with
nothing but priests and widows

and i have seen myself reflected in
the windows of abandoned buildings and
i have turned away

i have called my lovers by
the wrong name and then laughed
and listen

whatever you write is meaningless

you save no one but yourself
and even this is questionable

remember

god isn't a lie
but a punishment

think about whatever it is
you've done wrong

the sun is god's face bleeding down

six a.m. in the age of rain
and the streets of someone else's city
flooded and filled with corpses and
this is what it takes to make us
forget the war

this is a woman shot dead by her brother

someone's mother raped in a room
filled with broken glass and
what i'm waiting for is to either be
forgiven or forgotten

i have spent too many years
dragging the people i love through the
filth of priests and politicians

i have turned away from my children

have slammed doors in
their beautiful faces
but wait

christ was never meant to be a weapon

the truth is only a
less direct form of lying

without a an obvious enemy we have
only each other to hate

cage

some minor ghost in
another room

some forgotten act of violence

a fifteen year old boy
in the woods

his girlfriend
who he's just beaten to death with
a length of rusty pipe

and what the earth looks like
from where i sit
is flat

what my wife cries herself to sleep about
at night is my blindness
and listen

jesus christ was the
original navajo

the idea of slavery
can never be separated from the
idea of america

or what about my son?

four years old and beautiful and
already well-versed in the
concept of hatred

or what about phil ochs?

found at the end of a rope in
his sister's house
and the fact that there was nowhere
for any of us to go from there

the fact that the government
believes in nothing
beyond itself

ask ronald reagan
if he lost any sleep over those
first few thousand aids victims

ask all of the dead orphans in
all of the ruined churches
if it felt good to burn

say what you want until some
fucker with a gun decides
it's time for you to die

the sun, the clouds, the bottomless sky

this desperation
and this age of silence

these corpses found with
their hands
tied behind their backs

these nameless women and
these laughing holy men and
these children and if
some of them are yours
the world won't end

if the war is won
it doesn't mean it's over

can you even imagine
how many people don't give a shit
whether you live or die?

do you really believe that
any of these whores you've elected
would sacrifice their own lives
to save yours?

or this

he was getting high when
his girlfriend came over and
he was laughing at something she'd said
when the guy she was fucking
shot him in the chest

he was found behind the
wheel of a stolen car in a
bus station parking lot and i
remember smiling when i heard the news

and i have no use for god

have no faith in poetry

no patience for the sad
desperate scribblings of the weak and
the lame and i number myself
among them

i love my wife and my sons but
it means nothing
in the world of money and weapons

it means nothing in the rape camps
or in the shallow ditches where
the decapitated bodies of
pregnant teenage girls are dumped

and no one ever told lorca this
and look where it got him

no one promised you salvation
but you still believe it will arrive

you lock your doors while the
soldiers smash in your windows

you run naked and burning down
some pitted dirt road towards
a man who wants nothing but to
take your picture

the war is lost without any of us
ever knowing it had begun

manifest destiny: a literal translation

or this man
who kills a priest

the priest who
rapes young boys

and we were
never promised beauty
and were only offered hope
by liars

we built our houses on
the bones
of the slaughtered

called it democracy

waited for the
first walmart to open

gira

the yards filled with
weeds and broken toys

cigarette butts

dirty needles

the hammer of god held by
the clenched fist of
government

the face of god, burned

what i am is an asshole

a father and a son
and a man standing at a window
watching september rain pool
in the driveway

a ghost with teeth and
what i hate is poetry

poets

politicians

the way we all become whores
at some point

and maybe i'm
moving too fast here

maybe cobain was concerned with
more than his own pain and misery

i've heard this
kind of talk before

have listened to a junkie father
explain why he was a victim
and when he was asked if he knew where
his children were
he said that wasn't the point

said the past has nothing to do
with the present

and in the morning
i walk jonathon to the bus stop
and feel the last good heat of summer
wash over me

in the evening
i drive past the apartment where
a woman i never knew was
murdered by her lover

i consider how far faith
can take any of us

i consider the idea of fear
as a weapon

the idea of hope
as a bottomless pit

the way that nothing we say is
ever exactly the truth

the truth is a length of rope,
the past a tightening noose

fifteen years later and
the memory of this dog again

chained to a tree in front of
an empty house and
the noises it made in its throat
while i stood at the edge of
the road and watched

the name of the girl who said
she'd always love me

my eyes closed in a dark room

all of the hours i've wasted
waiting to feel this pure again

small moment of ascension in the
desperate season

sunday afternoon in this
house of dead mouths
with my wife and son asleep

my faith questioned by a stranger
while my left hand crawls slowly
across the
prophecies laid down by the right

and there is a moment
where the sun finds a gap between
the clouds and the hills and
the ordinary decay of this dead-end street
is suddenly transformed into
something beautiful
and there are the swaying bodies
of all the witches hung in
the name of god

history is meant to be ugly

what we learn
from the crucifixions and
the massacres is an addiction
to power

a contempt for the poor

and i am not a believer in poetry or
in the ability of words to
function as weapons

i was there
when the bleeding horse was
brought to its knees

i understand why
the weakest are chosen as
sacrifices

what i don't want to know
are their names

the written word disguised as truth

the women are raped
silently beneath a blue sky
in rooms with or without windows

this is always a part of
someone's history

the smell of burning flesh and the
photographs of the slaughtered and
in the here and now i am
cupping your breasts in my
sweatslicked hands

i am naming the stars and
blessing the spaces between them
and there is a day where i
realize i will no longer live forever

where my son
will see for the first time
the man i truly am
and turn away in shame

there are pages in history that
cannot be rewritten

but i have yet to see one

i include my own life here

the events that actually happened
and the ways they were changed in
                    the retelling
and i am no different from any of you

about this much
at least
i can be honest

it costs me nothing to
point out
that we will all drown together

opened her arms, said come home

And here along the river wall where
the teenage dogs spray paint FUCK in
bright grey letters, where the truth is
nothing more than what it pretends
to be, is the same here as anywhere else,
and the stench rising from the water,
the abandoned shopping carts, rusting
bones of small animals, plastic bags
caught in the underbrush, and then
what? The city can only spread like
a cancer or die like a victim. The
future is only a single crumbling wall
holding up a collapsing roof. I can't
remember a time in this place when
                    I wasn't afraid.

the necessity of pain and fear

beautiful and high in the
pure white light of the sun and
never anything to eat but
broken glass

never anything to break
but promises
and then the small white flowers
that blossom where the
pieces fall

the filth that we
bathe our children in

the men of god who would
have us beg for more

who would have us lose
all sight of joy

the poem is only a means of killing time

driving slowly
across the moonscape
this town becomes
in january

driving blind into
this afternoon glare filtered
through a skin's thickness
of grime and road salt
and is there anything here
that really needs
to be said?

has this life been nothing but
one unending afternoon
filled with the missing fathers
i called my friends?

and maybe
the sons of these men
will grow up happy or maybe
they'll just grow up to express
their anger with the same
tightly balled fists that
marked their mothers

maybe the daughters
will disappear

will repeat the
mistakes of their pasts
and there is nothing profound
in revealing the obvious

the poem is
only a means of killing time
until the light turns
green

the things
that truly matter were
never meant to be defined

hangman

you inside the sacred circle and
yr lover outside the door with
a bullet in his head

no small amount of magic

a mirror facing its darker twin and
then an infinite number of walls
inside the prison of your mind

a dream of your father and
of his father before him

an unbroken line of suicides

all those sad grey songs of
infinite joy that
no one ever sings anymore

the forest's edge and what we found there

your job is to map the
city of masks, but where to begin?

snow covers everything
and the stench of corpses

a war?

always and everywhere
                yes
   but this feels different

a plague maybe
or a loss of hope

the age of internet porn and
no way to escape it

a victim is a victim
no matter how many lies you tell
and the only way to be a
politician is to be a whore

the only way to fuck the
weak and the starving is to do it
until they bleed and then

do it again

why do you keep
begging for the truth if it's
never what you want to hear?

poem in the shadow of the bleeding horse

keep who you are
hidden

walk backwards down these
shadowed halls until
you find the room of hanged men

until the difference between
love and fucking finally
matters

far away

and this is the easy part,
the gun, the rope, the
hammer, just your own hands maybe,
and then you kill the child,
and then what?

try bringing it back
to life?

meditation on futility

or the boy who
shoots out the eyes of
dogs w/ his .22,
all grown up

the future suddenly
nailed to yr door and its
blood washing over
everything

a priest with his hands cut off standing in the
shallow light of god

in the broken years of marching
we believed

in the empty hand we placed our faith
and we were the shadows of birds
up the sides of dead buildings

we were the buildings with our
broken glass and our sunken parking lots
and the fields of poison where the
children played and listen

we weren't the children
but the parents

we dug the graves and spread the
prayers out like soiled blankets

we drank and fucked to give our
lives meaning and
in the morning we threw up

we apologized to strangers while they slept
and we got dressed

crawled out into the unbearable heat
of august with the taste of
broken glass in our mouths

with credit cards spilling from our wallets
and all of them maxed and the
houses that we knew all locked against us

and there was always the one who
spoke endlessly of killing himself and
on the morning he finally did it
we all acted surprised

we all acted concerned

and the soldiers were laughing in
those last seconds before the truck
plowed into the compound and exploded

the women were raped in the beds that
the corpses of their babies
had been kicked beneath

i remember seeing it on the news

i remember undressing you in the
bathroom of our apartment

crawling on the floor and singing like
starving dogs and
when the war was finally over there was
no one left to rejoice

there was no one to
give this precious freedom to

we opened our mouths to speak but
they were full of blood

church on fire

says *i'm sick of
this shit*

says *tell me a story with a
happy ending for a change*, and so i
paint her one of tanguy's skies
instead

i paint her one of
kahlo's visions

i drive over to the north side
to find her father, but
no one's seen him in
twenty years

no one gives a fuck about
the sixties, no one gives a shit about
lennon's murder, about reagan's
death, about anything other
than money or power

the past is empty nostalgia, the
future a fever dream of possibility
and i sleep on the couch
all week

i consider apologizing for
things i haven't done

in the end i keep quiet
and the infection spreads

the sun barely clears the hills to the
south on the coldest days of the year and
the air is thick with the smell of
gasoline, of metal grinding against
metal, and she says
    slow down

says *that was the exit* but the
trick is to get further away, out to
where the hills no longer have names,
out to where the trees rise up forever
dead from lakes of black water,
and the trick is to forget the children,
and the trick is to drive out past
even this, out past memory and
pain, but the truth is that the
trick always fails

the truth is that sex always
ends up feeling better
than love

isn't this what you've been
waiting to hear me say?

upstate landscape w/ minor premonition

or all of those days spent
waiting for something to happen

all of those wasted hours caught
beneath a pale white sun, beneath a colorless sky,
and it was always early afternoon and it
was always the middle of november

powerlines stretched from dying
house to dying house and
empty trees never quite casting shadows
across barren lawns

the highway and the back roads

endless empty spaces packed tight w/
the ghosts of the past

nothing subtracted from
nothing
again and again

::

the car out of gas on
fire at the edge of the highway the
swimmer alone late autumn or
early his wife missing
or sleeping
the children not yet imagined
and this car this wasteland this
all barren fields and powerlines all
empty stretches of interstate
mountains in the distance
and a man you might have
been always swimming
towards them

imaginary poem while waiting for rain

but this is only the day of
angels and we are only cities on fire

we are in the car for eight hours straight,
up and down side streets,
scoring and then using and then looking to score again and
what we smell like, i'd guess, is
slow meaningless death

what we believe in are better gods
or no gods at all
and the radio is tuned in to neverending static on the
morning your husband walks out the door

still gone four days later,
fucking someone's sister in a leaky trailer and
together they are only a monotonous story with a
predictable ending

a suicide that drags on for seven years

and her children sit and wait outside the
bedroom door, and this boy no one knows is found
alongside the interstate, raped and beaten and dead,
eyes gouged out, coat hanger wrapped
tight around his throat

fourth of july in this
age of casual oblivion

religion forced down your throat and
deep up into your ass and whoever tells you that
voting will bring about change is a liar

power will always be power and poverty a crime and
we have been walking lost through this forest
for days now or for a month or maybe for
half our wasted lives

i have told you i love you and i have
told you i hate you and
neither one is anywhere near the truth

i have tasted your sweat and i have
drunk your blood and i have
offered you mine and
we are dying stars in broad daylight

we are dirty needles on piss-stained floors

the truth sounds better as a metaphor and then
better still as a lie and the windows here
are all broken, the walls filled with
dead and dying bees

end of july

walk out the door and drive through
100 miles of nothing and then
100 more and then start to see a pattern

believe only in what you can hold

fall asleep at the highway's edge beneath
a relentless sun and
what the fuck were you thinking,
growing up, starting a family?

what the fuck were you
thinking, giving yourself away?

bought a house with no roof, no walls,
water in the basement

pulled the plug on your father

spoke quietly about your grandmother's suicide
in a roomful of strangers and none of them
listened and why would they?

this is the 21st century

age of emotional famine

age of indifference

wake up in the middle of frozen lake in
early february with a head full of
broken glass and think about summer

try to remember how you
ended up here

open your eyes for once in your life

the dominion of light, loosely translated

in the shadows of houses,
among the dead leaves and
broken branches, last ice of spring
shot through with dirt and ashes,
near the stump of the giant pine tree
that my ex had cut down five or six
years ago, plastic bag caught on the
rusting fence, fence more decorative
than anything, strands of it snapped,
lengths of it missing, poles bent
and the air here striving for warmth,
fighting against the wind that cuts
these quiet spaces in two, the bones
of small animals where the cats
have left them, woman across the
street calling for her daughter,
daughter somewhere safe i hope
but it's almost dark, it's almost
twilight, and i am always afraid,
am always cold and eventually
there are no more shadows, there
is only shadow, and we are all
feeling blindly for the names of
the things that we love

the world, awake

built you a poem of
wood and bone

a house of prayer
and ashes

said *you will wake up
naked in another man's arms*
and you did

said *the war will continue
long after everyone's
forgotten why it ever began*
and you laughed

hadn't yet been given
the box that held
whatever was left
of your son

words like black blood from the frozen ground:
a psalm

and twenty years later
you still dream of
your childhood house on fire

you turn to me for all of
the things i can no longer give you

the names of streets or of
old lovers or
the reassuring weight of lies
and everything we breathe is poison
because there are no other choices

are only dead trees lining the
edges of empty fields
and then the town i grew up in
with its stench of dead factories
and desperate bars

and somewhere in this poem
there is an afternoon of
blinding sunlight without heat

the sound of engines
grinding hopelessly against
a sky-blue sky

the shadows of hills crawling
towards highways
and what i forget in august is
the broken glass pain of december

the feeling of skin cracked and
peeling away from the bone

the taste of road salt
smeared across any flesh i
might hope to kiss

nothing built on
the ashes of your past

man drowning in a second story room

sunlight in january
but no shadows

a young boy
left to die in a locked room

i speak of this too often
i know
but can't shake the image

can do nothing but
spit on the idea of god
and listen to my son's quiet breathing
as he sleeps beside me

and i have walked away
from all of my friends
or they have walked away from
whoever i was at the time

i have spent too many hours
reading atwood's *morning in the burned house*
in the darkening light of early evening with
all of my small bitter possessions
gathered tight around me

we make noise for a reason
i say
but quietly
and st maria kisses my forehead

she understands how easily
faith
leads to desperation

holy poem, after the death of god

snow all afternoon but
nothing is made beautiful

no one is considered holy

at some point
the last city is built
and then there is only slow decay

sons are shot and
daughters raped and all of
the missing are given names
and some of them come home
while others are martyred

and there is always the threat of
another religion
of the crippled
leading the blind and
of a war that everyone can
believe in

a way to kill only the
truly deserving

how much of your life are
you willing to waste
making these decisions?

not the dream, but everything that comes after

sunday afternoon as
grey as the bones of christ
while the burning girl's
bones grow cold

while the sidewalks crawl
to the edge of town and then
all of the names for whatever
lies beyond

all of the ways love
might turn to violence

and i've given you the myth
a hundred times now
and what you're hungry for is
the truth

the reason a person
might open their mouth
then burst into flames and
all i can show you is
how easily an extended hand
becomes a fist

can you picture a man
chained to the back of a truck
then dragged to his death?

do you remember the
two young boys left to drown
while their mother
watched?

i offer you nothing
in place of your god

show me where
there's any difference

the blood factory, revisited

or maybe
the failure is mine
diane

maybe the words
are only words and
exist without blame and
maybe none of the battered wives
give a shit about poetry

this needs to be
considered

burying the sun

late september
and the cold is sudden
and each day shaped
like a fist and
every moment defined by
the disasters that have
brought us to it

do i move too fast here?

there is only
a certain amount of peace
to be found sitting alone in
an empty house all
afternoon

there is only
one song to be sung
when de chirico calls with
the news that he has discovered god

and at some point
the shadows eclipse the objects
they spill from

five o'clock becomes six
and the sky begins to darken

the voices of those who
discuss beauty
begin to fade

are replaced by the sound of
a crying child
or maybe only by the silence
after a door is kicked down
four minutes too late

after a tiny body
breaks the water's surface
far beyond the sight
of land

its eyes open and staring
not at god
but to an empty sky

the girl on fire tells you what she knows about love

which isn't much

which
when written down
looks like a blank sheet of paper

like a prayer offered up to
a god who isn't there

the ideas
of religion and brutality
inseparable

room filled with broken objects

a room filled
with broken objects in
a house
waiting to burn

is this what you dreamt of
as a child?

a man wearing
his funeral shoes and
an insincere smile

an empty bird cage

a sun without heat

any number of
meaningless objects that
add up to the same life
your mother lived and all the
baby does is cry

all the man does
is read the words of
dead south american poets

and pretend to
understand

and the difference between
cold and *numb*
is a subtle one when
everything you hold falls
through your fingers
to the floor

and the weight of the sky
is brutal
but necessary

you have
spent your life believing
this lie without
question

a pale yellow sun in a plain white house

the word is
god
and she has been making
her blood holy

she has been eating
the poisoned heart
of her unborn child

has been spreading
her scabbed legs in the
name of religion

and will you glorify the smell
of death that clings to an
eighteen year-old junkie?

will you love her if
i call her *christine* or
allison or *tami*
or have we moved too far
from the sun?

and imagine she has
parents

a pale yellow room
in a plain white house
somewhere in the midwest
to call her own
and yet here she is

a thin girl
just beginning to show
her pregnancy

a damaged smile filled
with too many teeth
as she walks towards you
with one dirty hand
held out

you will kiss it and
taste only pain

the poet runs out of words

this is the
room

the poet
run out of words
the carpet worn and
stained

and art is picasso

is hemingway is
dali

cold and dead
and still the wars
continue

meaningless
with the bodies laid
end to end in the
broken glass

mothers children dogs
and whores

and the poet watches
the empty street
for inspiration

waits for the
unexplainable pain
in his left wrist
to subside

wonders
if lorca thought
his blood was
actually being
spilled for
the good of
anyone

number 29, 1950, second attempt

these things seen
through sheets of glass
are almost real

think of history

understand that i would
place you against the
flawless blue sky and call you
beautiful

would pick at the same small wound
for thirty-eight years until it
came to define me

and i have spent my life
among men who claim to have found
god in a bottle

i have tasted
my father's ashes

will spend the rest of my life
hurting the people i love
and calling it art

all i ask is
that i be forgiven

to starve in a house we call home

and in these
thin shadows cast by
the darker half of the sun
even this cross looks
holy

simple lengths of wood
held together by pain
and there are those among us
who would let a man be
dragged to his death

there is the song you sing
quietly at midnight
when my hands find your heat
and what we never let
fall between us is
the word love

is the taste of your
best friend when she
knocks on my door at three
in the morning
or that the man downstairs
has been thinking too much
of the gun in the back
of his closet

calls his ex-wife
in the small hours
just before dawn and cries
and all it does is make
her boyfriend angry

all it does is wake
the baby up
and then at daybreak
it begins to rain

cold and hard and with
the shadows washed away
all that remains are the bones
of forgotten martyrs laid bare
down these broken glass
alleys

we will not be the first
to starve in
a house we call home

a footnote to the season of rust

a darker light
here at
the end of the day

all blue bled to grey
and the sudden failure of solid objects
to cast shadows

the flags hung
like condemned men

and our lives can no longer carry
the weight of secrets
and confessions begin to spill
from my clenched fists

begin to fall like ashes from
your perfect mouth

we have spent seven years
mourning the burning girl
without ever knowing her name

have both approached
the bones of christ from opposite ends
of the same empty field

and when you ask me if i regret
all of the friends i've lost
and i answer no
you think i might be
telling the truth

you understand too late that
i won't be
the man who saves you

and when you ask if
i'm sorry for any of this
i can only smile

stealing the title to atwood's *notes towards a poem that can never be written*

there is this need to
discuss pain

to describe
the color porcelain becomes
when it's smeared with blood

language i've been told
    is a gift
and on a wednesday evening
late in the season of weeping ghosts
one of the words you unwrap is
      loss

the space you stand in
falls somewhere between hatred and despair
and the sky is grey and hung only
inches above the rooftops

the walls tremble but hold

and when you pick up the phone and dial
maybe the word you speak into
your sister's waiting ear
will be decay

maybe the description you give
will be of two tiny arms
horribly deformed

what matters is that you
make her feel

the body dissected, the cancer laid bare (later)

each story is true

the woman's body is found
naked and wrapped in a dirty blanket
on some railroad tracks
eighty miles north of here

her left hand writes a
message on a bathroom wall
and she's saved at a truck stop in a
state i've visited

someone is caught
or not

my wife calls from
her sister's home and
mentions me in her list of fears

do you notice that the
story is over?

we've moved on
to less certain things

sit down she says
on a different day in another season
i'm pregnant

and i think of everything i have
and of everything i've lost
until it all gets confused

i think of diane looking for
the king of spain

and i have never claimed to have
profound insight

never claimed
to have divine wisdom or the
soul of a poet

i understand
the alchemy of loss into anger

i understand fear

tried for years to transform it
into something pure

was there when
the dress was found in a dumpster

and later that night i was drunk
on the hood of a car in a
field of tall grass

and there is no hidden meaning
in the deaths of strangers

the house burns or the car slides
into oncoming traffic or the
man grows tired of the
sound of begging

pulls the truck into a rest area
and leaves the engine running

thinks the thing through
without emotion
then does it

the collapse of the human cathedral:
a premonition

the meaningless noise of
unfinished thoughts all afternoon
and the shadows of clouds moving
slowly over the hills

wind down this street i live on
and the fact that what we think about
is leaving

what we talk about is nothing

not silence but the
small unimportant sounds we make to fill it

the simple agreement that
war is bad and
the unavoidable fact that it still
happens

and if not war then
the subtle collapse of things

the walls of this house cracked
the ceiling sagging and the way that
none of the rooms are ever warm

the pebbled window on the staircase
which lets in light without shape

everything familiar but i never feel at ease

the air is too bright here
the ghost of de chirico too heavy

and the statues on these lawns
should bleed or at least weep

i should have more faith
in the future but don't

the lack of possibilities is
a terrifying thing

building something darker in the ruins
of the human cathedral

all of these letters
from all of these delicate poets
and i am sorry for all of them but
have nothing to give

jesus christ never cared
about any of us

victor jara is gone

hands broken
and body butchered
and i find myself in a nation
full of priests who would
rape my son

i find myself looking for something
more permanent than belief

and there is a man who tells me
that my words all feel
like attacks

who says i might possibly
be forgiven but will never be
numbered among the blessed

and there is
the queen of open wounds
who says that all she ever wanted
was to be loved

there is her child and the man
who beats her and
all of the ones who wait
their turn

who among them
will be chosen
to wear the face of god?

a cold spring afternoon in the world
of darker truths

a flag and
the shadow of a flag
and everything in between

the smell of burning and the
sound of dirt falling on coffins
and all of my selfish reasons
for wanting to live

all of these houses wrapped tight
like shrouds around
all of these breathing ghosts

and if i find you in
the room of empty chairs
and you turn to me and smile
i will call it faith

if you give me the burning girl's name
i will hold it like the beating
heart of christ

this is love

this is the sound the springtime sky
would make if it could sing

and if you can't forget the war
then at least forget the fact
that children are dying

forget the fact that they
are taken from their homes by
men they've known their
entire lives and found
four days later in shallow
graves at the desert's edge

i've been told it can
be done

i've been told
that brutality is inevitable

this much
i think i believe

blue

here where
the streets all run
blue to the river

where the needle crawls
blind through
forgotten back yards
searching for the
one true vein

every one of these houses
is for sale
every one of these children
unwanted

and do you remember the year
of the burning girl?

it never ended
just spread from town to town
like beauty reversed

do you remember the
season of rust?

you do if

your sister lost her
unborn child
and maybe now you drink
too much

maybe you lock
the bedroom door and cry
while your own children
scratch to be let in

there is no future
so bleak it
can never come to be

indian summer

or october
which is the smell
of wet sunlight
on blacktop

which is the uneasy rush
of waiting to be
a father

of falling from an
impossible height over
some vague expanse
of wasteland

everything
suddenly beautiful
just when it no
longer matters

shaped by fire

she is less
than
what she was

she has been
shaped by
fire

has been
broken down
then put back
together and
no one is
holding
her

no one is
telling her
she's
beautiful

we are all
too busy
turning away

in the afternoon of bitter confessions

in the season of myths
i am empty

in the afternoon of
bitter confessions i remain
silent

these are the walls we
call home and
beyond them
the sky is white

the sun has lost something

is warm but only faintly
like an almost forgotten memory
and the trees all shimmer
beneath it

and the story is yours
and you tell it
softly

the suicide of a friend
or maybe the overdose
maybe the body found

shortly after midnight in any
pointless upstate town

the face black
the fingers rigid
around something

a steering wheel or a
bible or a pack of
cigarettes
and the air is sweet through
these open windows
and i am not
a compassionate man

am not the man you married

my eyes are pale green
my teeth white and even
my smile an angry thing

i could hold you
but don't

could tell you
a story of my own but
choose not to

i have become my
father's son

desperate poem from the season of rust

a small song sung softly
for this woman found
raped and strangled in her bed

an empty gesture
for the living
to comfort themselves with

take it with you
to the hill of fifteen crosses

take it to
the missing girl's door on
an overcast day in september
eight years after the fact

tell her parents that
you believe in redemption

tell them that the spirit holds
more weight than the bones

realize finally
how worthless your lies
really are

myself a bastard son

what i give you is the world
in terms of cancer

people devoured
and objects destroyed
and the simple truth that there
is no cure

that the children next door
stand on the side of the street and
dare each other to touch the
decomposing remains of
a small animal

and this is nothing new

it's where we've come
from the burning of witches and
the lynching of slaves

it's the idea that democracy
by itself
is enough to save us

and i believe in love
yes

but i believe in money too

i believe that beauty
can only be defined by the ugliness
that surrounds it

consider that every year of your life
has been defined to some extent
by war

by the deaths of both
loved ones and strangers

and in the kitchen
the faucet drips and
in the back yard
a cautious version of the sun
appears

the faint shadows of
buildings and of trees

the sound of an airplane

the sky
suddenly luminous with
possibility

letter to kurt cobain, seven years dead,
on his 35th birthday

fuck this
idea of heroes

fuck this idea
of gods
of any kind

do you agree?

do you
believe?

i can't hear
you

the moment with clarity, but no definition

or else the boy
walks into his house
to find his brother murdered

his mother dead by
her own hand

blood everywhere
but nothing spelled out

nothing left whole or
recognizable

the future enormous

faith in nothing: a confession

or the smell of slowly
decaying houses
in these first warm days of fall

the unthinking weight i place
on chelsea's heart

and what i can't
seem to shake are the
last meaningless words i spoke to
this man i know before he
went home and put the gun
in his mouth

do you understand that
i'm human?

it becomes harder to prove
with each passing year as the list
of people i would call friends
grows smaller and smaller

and did i have a childhood?

of course
but i can't seem to make
any connections between

the boy i was and the
man i've become

and i continue to
write these poems but what
any of them actually say
is an uncertain thing

what any of us choose
to do in the face of tragedy
seems irrelevant

i know i'm not the
only one to accept this
as truth

black chalk

or when the sunlight
tastes like gasoline or where the
clouds gather into fists
above the hills

this woman i know who
says she loves me but
that she won't leave her husband

won't walk to the edge of the field
where the child has been bound
and shot and
if there's a truth i would have you know
it's that the war cannot be stopped

these men who have written their
names in blood on the courthouse wall
are the biggest kinds of assholes

are as useless as poets and
if i were in california
i would be kneeling at the feet of
saint maria

i would have
no more use for words

would forget the feel of salt rubbed
into cracked and peeling skin
the sound of metal grinding against
metal on ten-below afternoons
and i would learn to forget
my children's names

i will learn to build
the holiest of towers from their
tiny bones

we are nothing without
this vast empty space between
joy and pain

sparrow

white-out afternoon in
the first days of spring

all distances the same

all answers multiplied by zero

wake up hungover to find
the baby's dead or your lover missing

windows shot out and all that
frozen silence pouring in

'92 i think or '93 and
i was in love with your sister
but sleeping with her best friend

was waiting for someone's husband to
kick in the door and my hands
were on fire with infinite vision

words scarred the furniture,
stained the walls, the
spaces between us, and i knew i was
the resurrection

knew i was down to my last
handful of pills and it was then and
then it became now

the dogs are sick and they're
starving but the baby's name has
been forgotten

the divorces have been finalized
and the river frozen over

we lost the war we couldn't lose and
then we crucified the doubters

grew up think summer would
never end until the morning we
woke up old and we have
no fear but this fear for ourselves

overdosed nurse in the back seat
of your brother's car and
you learn to wear hope like a noose

i pull the shades,
i get undressed, i lie down
beneath the dining room table

we are forever fucked without our
empty, fleeting pasts to
nail us to this here and now

we are nothing and nothing can save us

and despite everything we've
created we are still surrounded by emptiness

we have the promise of the lottery

we have ipods for
starving children everywhere

and it feels good to rest out here
to just drop to your knees on the edge of
burnt hill road and let the blood flow,

and it feels good to close yr eyes

left him lying there because the baby was
crying, buzz of flies was a soft blanket,
a wall, a gentle ocean

shadows of birds in flight

could taste it, like music or the
sound of running feet

no one asleep, but one of us turned away

autumn maybe or the end of summer
and the heat like a dull blue shroud

silver sun in a sky the color of dust and
despite all of the wars we'd won
we were lost

found the mother in a shallow grave with her
hands cut off but we never found the father

had 400 channels to choose from
and it wasn't enough

had some good fucking medicine

still hated myself, but not as much

not as fiercely

missed the heat that came with
all of that glorious empty anger

bird imagery 2

like a body found hanging
from the
underside of a bridge

like dirty white skies or the
rusted metal towers that
grow from the ridges
of anonymous hills

wherever you are
it's always 20 years too late

whoever you wanted to be
we always end up nothing more
than hungry ghosts in the
age of crows

saints nailed to crosses
in upstate fields and
the man said sing
and so we did

said jump because it was
only the 98th floor

because it almost
felt like flying

broken hand w/ mirror

in this world where
almost everything is beyond
your control and your
choices are limited to false
god, slave, impotent king

vote or don't vote
shoot or don't shoot and
        either way
the starving continue to starve

grow old
then

die

eat handfuls of dust

send postcards back to
your loved ones, to
your enemies

let them see you
        finally
for the empty threat you
        always were

blue skied surrender

you near an ocean
      not my own
and what we have between us
          is silence

choices are made
absences explained

you tell me not to tell you there was
never any hope
but what does it matter?

i have these pictures
and my faith in sunlight

the train tracks here
echo the curve of the river

men with the heads of carrion birds,
with fangs and claws,
live in the trailers up in the hills

money is power and
      power is god

death is death, but there are
better and worse ways
to approach it

i choose running away

choose willful blindness

have only ever been brave
when there was nothing
valuable at stake

postcard to california

and you and i like
forgotten kings cutting wires,
like ghosts in empty fields

you and i staring
blindly into the sun

drowning, but slowly,
five years and then ten,
blood turned to amber,
empires to dust and
then you and i like
open flames

you and i like ashes

all of the years we will
spend growing cold

splendour

grow up fearing
men w/ answers

grow up fearing
growing old

reach the age at
which you are
no longer any use to
        anyone

sit beneath the
dull yellow heat of
august skies and
consider suicide

consider sleep

the fear of dreams

of waking up
one day closer to
        winter

of not waking up
at all

into view

not blindness
but the sky gone dark

porch lights

bitter wind

in any story, you
are only the sound of
dead leaves down
sleeping streets

in any dream, i am
only the moment
of despair

you wake up
sweating and see with
absolute clarity how
all of our kingdoms
will fall

one for j

wake up heavy with the
idea of suicide on some bright
blue july morning and
        then what?

you need to look in all
directions here

you need to consider hope
         vs
  the possibility of hope

your children as a
form of salvation

  salvation as a concept that
        might
actually have some meaning

ash wilderness

the edges of cities
where the bodies are buried

the sides of hills and
the scrubland on either side of
the highways

and it matters that i love you
but not enough

it makes its own grey logic
that the killers need
to be killed

ask any parent
how old their child
would've been and then
look at their hands when
they answer

look at your own

use them to dig out
whatever space you can find
between anger and despair

a forest

growing up quietly,
invisibly,
or this is what you thought

growing up without limitations
and then dying

write your name
      backwards
in the book of crows

hang a cross in
front of every mirror

religion, yes, and then
superstition
and then genocide

all acts
are acts of greed

all apologies are
acts of violence

baby just lies there bleeding
and all you can do
is keep saying *i'm sorry*

the village, on fire

my youngest son crying over
the idea of my death and i
have no idea how we've
arrived at this point

i have no more reasons
to hate my own father

feel nothing but fear when
i consider the future

five years and then ten and
then twenty tied down by
the need for money.
        for shelter,
        for food,
        for money again

day one in the
age of addiction

white sun in a silver sky

houseful of broken windows,
of leaking pipes and
unread books

my youngest son in tears,
which is suddenly
the source of all pain

notes on finding religion

We were silent while the
boat sank. I think I've
mentioned this. Land in the
distance off to the west, blinding
sunlight, and it wasn't
enough just to be in love

and it never is

and we never were

and the boat was sinking

miro was dead

Couldn't understand why none
of the things I had spent my
believing in never really
mattered in the end.

the sick child in a room filled w/grey light

and rain in the palace of leaning bones
and the fields all thick with mud
              with grey weeds
           and garbage
and there is only ever where you are

leaking roof
and a man with a gun

homicide or suicide but at
least the baby sleeps through it

the sun is a rumor spread by
maria out on the west coast

you want to believe her
but the car won't start

your fingertips crack and bleed

the poem is no more or less a
waste of time than anything else while
we wait for the weather to clear

leonard sends news of another dead poet

midnight in the palace of
leaning bones and
you sleep poorly

rain down the walls, staining
the pictures, blurring them, phone
almost ringing but not quite and
in the dream your oldest
son was dying

awake
you're paralyzed,
afraid to walk across the hall,
afraid to look too closely
in the mirror

not as old as your father yet,
but older than cobain

older than christ

useless accomplishments in a
world already
overflowing with them

max ernst, all is forgiven

cold in the shadows down these side streets
and the flicker of sunlight
through bare trees

the names of people whose names
i will never know

the churches and the waves of desperation
that radiate from them

i've never asked for salvation
never wanted forgiveness

the world is full of children dying slowly
behind locked doors,
is full of priests with their precious words
that taste like dust
and when i tell you that the storm has passed
it doesn't mean that any of us
should come out of hiding

when i tell you i love you
it's almost never out loud

what this feels like is safety

the indifferent heart

kept telling my father
he was dead
but the fucker wouldn't listen

a generation of drunken car crashes
giving way to
a generation of heroin slaves,
a neverending stream of pathetic suicides,
and it was my mother who found him
on the kitchen floor

it was my sister who made the
prophecy from 3000 miles away

sent a letter from the church of st. maria,
sent a box of bones,
a postcard of some anonymous couple
fucking on the beach at sunset,
and i told my father
he was dead

told him he was an asshole,
the two of us standing there in the
wreckage of our shared past,
and my mother said
leave him alone

said it was all a mistake

sister told me i was an asshole

laughed when her boyfriend
kicked her down the stairs

kept telling him he was dead no
matter how hard he hit her and i was
2000 miles away, dreaming of
being in the arms of st. maria

told my wife i didn't
love her anymore and she laughed

told me i was an asshole

gave me a list of my failures and
it was her boyfriend who called the
next day to tell me my
father was dead

it was the sound of my mother
crying in the next room

my sister,
5000 miles away,
screaming

no luck, only slowly dying machines

can't just sit in the
corner swallowing your own blood
                            forever

can't be a prophet when you have
                nothing to say
                so just shut up

just stand there laughing
holding handfuls of fire for the
starving children to eat

know that i love you and then
know that i hate you and that the
                stars are all dying

should one of us care?

will either of us ever grow
cold enough to
put the other in the distant past?

seemed like a possibility once
the sunlight all turned
to snow

the sky, blatantly

With your unused coupons,
with your losing lottery tickets,
not raped but beaten,
on the floor and bleeding,
a baby crying in another room,
a man with a question,
a cop,
asks how long ago it happened,
asks why no one here stepped forward
to save Christ,
and the room is a cell,
one of the walls is made of bars,
and you're naked,
tied to a cot,
and the stranger with the gun wants an
answer that you don't have.

Your arms have been broken.

Your tires have been slashed.

Man at the door says he loves you
just before he kicks it down.

painting a poem for ernst, who was never
my father

and i'm thinking there are
                reasons
and then i'm realizing there aren't

moments maybe
which become moments wasted

apologies spoken inaudibly
        spoken 20 years too late and
        to the wrong person

addictions

locked rooms

early afternoon but getting dark
and it's almost winter at the
forest's edge when you find the child

you wave to each other and
then turn away and
one of you is never seen again and
the other is never forgiven

this is what i mean, this
lack of oxygen, this invisible weight
that pins me to the floor

these men with the
heads of wolves

you want to scream as you
watch them approach
but there's no air left to breathe

an accumulation of ghosts

    sunlight and
    this man in his
    front yard
    his children watching
            him burn
    watching him die
    and sunlight
    shimmering on pools in
    bright green back
    yards and this
    man this one brief
    moment this soft
    sigh of regret
    this relentless crush
        of passing days

his later years

grow up and then
lose direction

move through wilderness

arrive at nowhere

no one tells you this
but all of them will laugh
once you've figured it
out for yrself

you'll be given a
drink or a gun

a map printed
white on white

enough goddamned good
will to last you until
the day you die

poem while watching dali paint
the iridescent sky

in the absolute heat,
in the shadows of trees,
           of empty houses,
this silence built from soft breezes,
from freeway traffic on the
other side of the river

this moment defined by
sunlight on chrome

by the absence of all pain

spend your lifetime buried
beneath belief and the loss of
faith becomes inevitable

dig at your flesh to try and
find the better person trapped
down deep inside and all you do
                is bleed

what i said to gorky

married the actress and then
she shot her father and
the movie was a hit

the song wouldn't end

ten minutes and then twelve and
it was fueled by poison but
no one said *no*

all of us with shovels and
hammers in a back yard
overrun with weeds

all of us in love
with the widow's sister

took turns fucking her until
the alarm went off,
already 80 degrees at eight in
the morning, didn't matter that the
roof leaked when the only thing
spilling in was heat

didn't matter about
my girlfriend's abortion, about
her father's heart attack, about
all of the starving children
in the world

i was 25 and drunk and
christ wasn't coming back

poem for a year of election

or like the
laughter of dogs

the ease with which
             zealots
murder their children

you will not
you cannot
but then you do

why cry?

the ideas of
WINNING and LOSING
are beaten into us
all from birth

every room in every
sanctuary is stacked
floor to ceiling with
the butchered corpses
            of victims

the cause no longer
matters when the
power feels this
goddamned good

icarus, one last time

that was the thing

naked and beautiful,
even then and even there and
even later with the cameras rolling and
the ropes tied too tight

visions of saints and
then the roof opens up and the
sky explodes and the man has a hammer
                        has a knife
                        has a gun

and the story isn't mine
but there's no one else here
and it was o'keeffe who said this,
but not to me and not to you
and not in so many words

it was late afternoon and
the buzz of insects was everywhere

the voices of patriots

drunk and then stoned and it starts
off as a joke but then gets
crippled by anger

it starts off with the rope and with
fists, with four against one and the
woman forgotten in a corner, and then
it ends up 400 miles later with
chains, with a pile of rags and bones
and a lot of talk about how the
bastard died hard

about how there really wasn't
anyone else to blame

with tired eyes

even here in the clean cold light of april
in the solemn emptiness between berkshire & speedsville
between somewhere & somewhere else
between nowhere & nowhere
the shit of civilization pokes up through the rocks and dirt

cigarette butts bottle caps burger wrapper

crisp blue sky

no sound of traffic or of industry but
two empty beer cans and a broken bottle off the side of
a rutted dirt road

taste of rust when i turn to kiss you

birds
screaming

why every poem should be the last one

july and this
abundance of weeds, these
vines growing without pause or
regret, smothering and strangling beneath
the flat silver glare of the sky, and
were we drunk?

are we stoned?

takes a handful of pills just to
make me feel normal in the morning

took fifteen years to peel away all the
dead flesh and then all i was
was fifteen years older

sounds like a joke
but the punchline needs work

sounds like a song written from
a great distance and with
broken hands and she says *listen*

she says
just let him die

july and the
heat of the railroad tracks

the buzz of empty fields

insects and generators and children
sleeping off sicknesses, fans in
curtained rooms and, outside, the broken
toys all faded plastic and splintered
wood, all rusted metal and here,
now,
year of the bleeding horse,
fever dream of my father's last hours,
i want you to know that i
forgive no one

i want you to know that i
have made peace with myself

i cast this shadow down these cracked
and buckled sidewalks, over patches of
warm tar, and i am afraid of
everything that exists beyond my control

i am choked with the fear of
all my failures

can remember the two of us in love beneath
the absolute weight of the summer sun
but can't seem to make it matter

without a name, without armor

old man in the corner of a sunlit
room and this is the future, yes, and
this is the past and the important
thing is not that i'm afraid but
that i'm tired

the important thing is that no one
should ever admit defeat
without first learning the history of war

no one should live in a shack
without electricity, without running water,
with the stench of corpses glued tight
to every waking minute and when i
tell the old man this
he laughs

when i ask about the end he says
he only remembers the beginning

says he was young

says it was a different room

doesn't believe me when i
tell him he's my father

seems pretty goddamned
sure of himself

inwards

says this says *we
are in god's fields* and holds
out her hands to feel the
falling snow but i'm
not so sure

i have seen the tire ruts
fill with blood

i have heard the crippled preach
have heard them claim there
is no bravery in slaying ghosts

have listened to the mothers of
weeping daughters as they
explained my failures

found myself
agreeing with them

found myself in this field
middle of december
storm approaching
and she says *the trick is to
never go straight for the eyes*

she says *the trick is*
to come up from behind

kisses the spot where the
knife would be driven home

man crawling on the ocean floor

sick of myself at 4 in the afternoon

ice on the shadowed sides
of sleeping factories

weeds

no news from god since
before i was born
and then the death of his only son
played out for cheap entertainment

this is the world you inherit
and then it becomes
the one you pass down

these are the dreams you dream
after your lover leaves

daughter was only three years old
was filled with cancer
and the sunlight was a lie

the moment approached and
then it passed and
the fear is what remains

nothing is revealed

nothing is given away

listen

in the moment of truth
there is only silence

in silence
there is only the sound of rain

all distance matters until you
cross it and finally know
yourself to be lost

lullaby, for beth

or here in the wilderness where
the houses turn themselves inside out to
reveal animals fucking children on
           garbage-strewn floors

where the sky has no color

where the roofs collapse and the
basements fill with water

a stranger's house and so you
sleep in a stranger's bed
and dream of escape

spend your money on poison

drive away finally on the coldest day of
           the year and
when your car breaks down like
you knew it would you
continue into the west on foot naked and
           blindfolded until you feel the
           sun begin to warm your skin
pray
if it makes you feel better

sing if it
keeps the past from rising up
to devour the future

call me when you finally grow
tired of christ's neverending pain

the ascension

this feeling you get
when you read about
rothko's suicide
or dee dee's overdose

this world of young girls
on their hands and knees while
the cameras roll

while the wars are fought
and the soldiers cut off
the feet of the smallest children

this
and the phone ringing
at some point in the afternoon
on easter sunday

your mother
eight hundred miles away
saying she's found your father

saying he doesn't remember
how he got there

a frightened man in
an anonymous hospital room
and what he wants is a drink
and a cigarette

what he wants is to
forget again

what he says is
take me home

each dog needs a name

the poems are dogs
and
the hand holds the whip

this feels true

and each dog needs
a name
and each face a scar
and some of us are
more willing to give than
receive

others
tilt their heads back
eagerly

expose the throat like
a sacred gift

wait to see the future
in whatever pours
from the wound

boy found dead in the river's veins

february and
the baby is hungry

they are all stoned in
the other room,
the sunlight pale and
without heat

cold
but brilliant
like the blind eye of god
and i have begun measuring
my life in failed
relationships

have been dreaming of california
and of the holiness that
radiates from the
pacific coast highway

and what i know is the smell
of fear,
the golden haze of gasoline,
and the name of the boy
found dead in the river's vein

and no one asks
to be christ here but
the nails are still driven home

there are men who
smile with the sharpened teeth
of animals and
there are the daughters
they rape and i am tired of
hearing that these words
i choose to give you
cannot be poetry

i am tired of the baby's screams

it was never enough
just believing we would all
become beautiful in some
unforeseeable future

carver's bones

what my hands
want to do is plunge
into the white light

wash themselves
clean of poetry while
carver's bones crawl the floor
in search of a perfect
word

and what is it
we try to say to each other
in these moments of
silence?

how many afternoons did we
waste stoned
while the baby slept?

remember

i have seen you buried beneath
mountains of regret

i have walked the hill of
fifteen crosses

without feeling the presence
of god
but the fault may be mine

each day wants to
spill across the fields
colder than the one before,
and when there's nothing
left to burn
all we'll have is love

this is not a fate i
recognize as my own

entropy

and at some point
you will wake up to
find a swastika painted
on your front door

you will be given
a definition of god

will be asked
to denounce your own

and how much
of what i describe here is symbolic
and how much is literal?

i can take you to the woods
where the cheerleaders
were murdered,
can show you
the missing girl's house
and wait while you ring the bell

i want to know how
her parents would measure
something relatively simple
like seven years but don't
have the balls to ask

i want to believe
the son of a bitch who
says he buried her bones

want to imagine
his last seconds will be
nothing but absolute
terror and blinding pain

i am a religious man
in my own way

first poem from the season of fear

september
without warning

a man i know has left
his wife and boy
for a married waitress with
three children of
her own

a car burns in
the breakdown lane on I-88

the days fall together in this way
with a late summer sun
hanging always over the hills
to the north

with the news of minor tragedies
meaning less and less,
and i'm reminded of
the suicide queen's father on the
day of the abortion

how he shook my hand and looked away

and i'm reminded of my sister
and all the bruises she
never spoke about

there is a need
for beautiful words to place
against all of this anger we endure
but my mouth is filled
with ashes

my hands are cold on
the steering wheel when the woman
on the radio tells me that the
east coast is in flames

that the innocent are burning
with the guilty

all of their screams
as terrible as the sound of
anyone's god

no blood no feathers

and she writes me
about
the color of the sky

about the silence
of the aftermath

a body in an
intersection

no blood
no feathers falling
from the wings
of angels

death small enough to
hold
in her hands,
and in this
infinite moment of
total clarity
she understands the pain
of being alive

understands the need
for it

and her sky is
all i see when i
close my eyes

poet as crow/as starving dog/as himself

somewhere between
day and night

somewhere between
home and lost

the 20th century dead and
picasso with it
and pollock all but forgotten

my father's ashes
on a shelf in a room i
no longer walk through

a letter in my pocket from
a man who says
*i don't like what you write but
feel that it's necessary*
and what i send him is this poem
written in a moving car

words that define nothing
but that move towards the hills
at a terrifying rate

this illusion of motion
and all of the reasons it's
necessary

all of the places i arrive at
without welcome

the news i bring
which is never good

driving back from the coast

something on the radio, neil young
maybe or the stones, and she says *god
i can't stand this shit* and
shuts it off

the next 30 miles spent considering
how simply the world falls apart,
and then the 20 after that,
and then we find the man w/ the axe
in his skull

we ask the left side of his face
where he's going, but it's
the right side that answers

says *home* in the voice of god

smiles, and the blood pours down
his shirt

shirt says SILENCE = DEATH

not that talking's ever really
saved anyone's ass, either

pyrrh

in the temples as they crumbled,
in the year of burning children,
where hands were windows,
where eyes are open,
saw shadows like scars,
felt the warmth of yr mouth,
kissed the salt from yr breasts

stood in the doorway
after the rain had passed

stood between yr husband
and his lover

called it the year of broken wings
   because none of us could leave,
because we could only fly in
                  circles,
could only repeat our mistakes
        again and again,
and when you turned to me i
   saw shadows like scars,
kissed the salt from yr lips,
felt the heat of yr lies

stood in the doorway after
the house we never shared had
burned to the ground

tora

said sorrow is easy and
then i showed you how

said *lennon is dead* said
d boon is dead said
cobain is dead and it was only
your face that changed and it was
only your name

it was winter

it had always been winter

a tired furnace in a
drafty house

the color blue but smudged,
                        dirty,
faded at the edges and you
took off your clothes,
said you were tired,
lay down naked on the ice

said you were bored and then
asked when i was
going to take you back home

after the age of enlightenment

not alone and not
dead, which is something

ask creeley

ask diane

play your copy of disintegration
until the walls no longer matter,
until the bright january
sky is all you can see

be yourself
despite the fact that
it's not enough

stand in the field where
beauty comes to die

feels so goddamned good just
breathing that you can't imagine
what it will be like to
finally stop

all hope edged w/ frost

and not warm yet and still the
scars and still the ghosts

shadows of empty buildings laid out
across the snow and frozen mud and the
song of light is only in your mind

the women weep at the river's edge

the baby is passed from one to the next

not war and never peace and
these is nothing worth dying for in this world
but it's always been so easy finding
reasons to kill

eagle flies up to the sun

man pulls the trigger and
brings it back down

boy sleeps in his bed of flames
while his mother drives away

nothing to do but map out all of
this hatred and pain and
hope that your own children can
find their way home

a gift, belated

rain down ghostwhite walls, all
static all fear just waiting for the roof to fall,
said take my hand, said slower
but the children were gone

    the lies all made sense

spoke each one like a bitter mantra
until my mouth filled with blood

watched christ in his agony and
then cobain, and i remember my father
telling me that it wasn't WHO you
hated that mattered but WHY

i remember his house on
the morning he died

the shadow of falling snow across
dirty windows, and she said
none of this matters if i love you

she held her mirror up to
the sun and laughed

felt strange when the
moment of joy refused to fade

unfinished film about prison

standing there on the rim of the valley
at the edge of the highway
and silent

emptiness and fear and
in the distance (in any direction)
a city

buildings where they sway and collapse
and huts made of straw and
the promise of burning witches

the smell of it
and the heat

like hope but
safer

the well of knowledge

they kill the father
and then his eight year-old son
which makes sense
if you want to rule out the
possibility of vengeance

they kill the mother
but not before they rape her

they save the daughter for
another day

on the occasion of my four year-old son learning
how to draw a peace sign

i am sitting here
thinking about sitting here

thinking about the photos of
all of those paintings of krasner's
that no longer exist

i am thinking
of course
about pollock

about myself and my wife
and our children

the need for beauty
in the face of pain

and i'm reading a letter
sent to me by a woman i know

something about a crack addict
beaten by her boyfriend

about the baby she gave birth to

i am reading the part where
she writes this story makes me
think of you

and what i feel is tired

what i refuse to believe in
is america

the strip malls
and the funeral homes
and the bloodthirsty smiles of
politicians

the carefully trimmed nails on
the hands of the priests who have
raped your sons and daughters

and i am sitting here thinking
about all of the unpaid bills
on the kitchen counter and about
how the walls of this house
hold no heat

i am waiting
for one war to begin or for
another to begin

for the first soldiers
to be flown home in bags

the words
spoken over their graves
which none of us will
remember

blood in the spaces between what we say
and what we mean

crows in an empty field

not the idea
but the fact of it

the sky with a
beginning and an end

the earth moving
beneath your feet and thick with
the bones of indians and
slaves

anywhere

whatever day it is in
whatever year
and all of the unpaid bills that
keep you tied to this life

all of the people you've hurt
who'd like to see you dead

the names you've forgotten and
the lovers you've betrayed

and the trees all bare

the sound of the freeway

the smell of cold engines
going to rust

of the rivers filled
with oil and sludge

america at this exact moment

a woman beaten unconscious
and left in the closet of a burning house
and the simple fact that i've
outlived cobain

have outlived christ and
that i refuse to die like pilate

and what about this
eighteen year old girl naked
except for a string of pearls?

how many wars are you
willing to wage just to own her?

not action
but the act of demand it
from others

all of these young men shot dead
for reasons that have more
to do with money than freedom

all of these songs with
words but no meaning

it was never enough
just knowing how to hate

halcyon

so tell it straight
then,
without the false romance of
distance and loss

you were in love
and then you weren't

you lost each other
found each other again maybe
then waited to see what
would happen

got by for a while on
sex and fear and memories
and then it wasn't enough

closed your eyes and
when the morning light forced
them open again
ten years had passed

you were both
married to strangers

you were both lost in
the forest

the edges had already
begun to burn

things that can burn

or consider what can
be said without words

believe in the spaces between us

twenty years of silence and of
cities in ruins

a lifetime of
dogs chained to fences

of horses starved and beaten and
what i believe is
that christ has forsaken us

what i believe is that everyone dies
frightened and alone

a man asks
do you know who you are?
and all lennon can do is stare
at the sky

bleed his life out onto this
filthy goddamn sidewalk

dream everything backwards to
some hopeful, lost beginning

golgotha, which is always within

threatens rain all afternoon and
the screams of crows
and then silence

that i miss you

that the killer nails the girl's hands
to the floor

that he burns down the trailer
after the act has been committed

these spaces between us
too much like cancer

in the joy of small truths

i have been trying to
name this feeling all day

have been waiting for the phone to ring,
for my children to call,
and i want to tell them that i love them

i want to
tell them that it matters

i want to hear them laugh at
how foolish i've become

desire

forget your fate, your fear of parasites,
the broken arms of winter. remember the
simple holiness of being eighteen. a time
before the devouring began, before the
machine was built, was perfected, was made
to run on pain and fear and human blood.
two friends dead of cancer by thirty, another
one a suicide. a fourth was just standing
there in the store, was shot dead with a bag
of chips in his hand. shot dead by a man who
would end up killing himself six hours later.
shot dead with a girlfriend back home, a
baby, and you never really knew him, but he
was eighteen too, was immortal, and you
need to remember this. you need to escape
the life you've built while you can. you
need to run.

shiva's blues

the broken hands of minor saints,
the unfinished thoughts. you curse
jesus, but to no avail. he's not
listening. he has his own problems.
can't get a record deal, but his face
is on every empty billboard between
here and fresno. park your car by
the side of the road. genuflect.
could almost be a picture of elvis,
if you were standing at just the
right angle.

first portrait of st maria in the style of dali

You in this sepia-toned photograph,
with your arms wide open in greeting,
with your hands held up in surrender.

Edge of highway, corner of house,
hint of something better. A body of water,
maybe, or the back of someone else's
head.

A gun pulled from inside the
killer's heart, and he says *Mr. Lennon,*
then smiles, then pulls the trigger.

No.

I've gotten ahead of myself here.

I'm ten years old and in a boat with
my father and two of his friends, and the
engine has died. the tide is going out,
and the only sound is the pull
of the ocean.

The only heat is the
mindless glare of the sun.

I don't know you yet,
haven't fallen in love with you,
haven't let my tongue flicker lightly
across your nipples in a
curtained room.

The story is over,
or is possibly just beginning.

I have the picture, but can never
make out the expression on your face.

a room of truths, a house of rage

dead man will fuck you hard,
will ride god's flaming stallion over the
corpses of yr children and call it justice and
if the landscape can only be painted w/ blood then
           there are decisions to be made

there are junkies to crucify and
politicians to hang for the tentative
promise of a brighter tomorrow

there is a nation of victims just waiting to
blame you for their problems but
screw that

draw strength from their misery and learn to
drink the marrow from their bones

understand yrself to be the enemy
           and laugh

easter

you alone in
the house of truths

the news of twelve soldiers
ambushed and slaughtered

the news of bodies being
set on fire and
dragged through city streets

and not the sun but almost

not warmth but
the memory of it

the snow melted and
the streets grey and the screams
of animals caught in traps

the blurred reflections of strangers
in the windshields of empty cars

all of these words and all of
these images that refuse to
add up to anything more than

themselves but you still have to
stop and consider each one

you still have to dig
until the bodies are found

it shouldn't take much longer
than the rest of your life

not the end of everything, but still

crows on a roof worrying bones
in the early-afternoon rain

just this
just silence shot through with
the hum of powerlines

a meaningless sound
like the voice of god

a question of so much
flesh & blood gone missing

new poems

recent past and unforeseeable future

and everything lost, and nothing ever found

ask *but what if i stop*
           bleeding?
and she laughs
           says
that's not gonna happen
and then turns up the volume

and maybe we are always
dying in small ways
and maybe that's normal

maybe a shallow grave out by
the edge of the interstate for
the rapist's daughter

a small wooden cross and a
bouquet of plastic flowers

all of the fear from my
childhood still wrapped tight
around my crippled heart
40 years later and i think i've
grown up to be the coward
my father always
told me i was

i think there should be more
than taking pleasure in
the pain we cause each other

it seems like i've been
wrong before

a new testament

and i am not your lost dog
            motherfucker
and this will not be the year of my death

we have been through it all before
                    you and i,
the colors of christ,
the subtle power of disco,
of drano and nyquil and a steady diet of malice and
what else can we do but live on a steady
diet of our favorite untruths?

who can you blame in the end
but the government?

think i told you before that we
gotta start back at zero

think we agreed that
sorrow was no substitute for vengeance

that justice always means more when it's
spelled out in the blood of
those who abuse their power

in the aftermath of the assassination
of the false king

but the child you were is gone

the stranger you've become means
nothing to any of us

the windows in this house all
thick with dust
and then streaked with rain

late november

early january

crows and stray dogs and missing children

grey on grey, like all great art

your lover where she falls asleep and then
fifty miles away, another slowly collapsing house
in another dying factory town, where
she wakes up

pass her the needle or pass her the gun

a mouthful of ashes for breakfast
                either way

a ringing in your ears

a heart that beats without logic, without rhythm,
and the doctor says its nothing you
can't learn to live with

says all lives end in death anyway
so why complain?

take what you have and run

move past your sister's suicide and out into
these dull brown fields
full of drunks and starvation artists

crawl up burnt hill road to the house of
the first girl you ever fucked,
but her mother says she's gone

says she never really lived there,
says she's forgotten her face, and i
remember all those years i spent
as a moving target

remember building cathedrals to
other peoples' gods, but that type of shit doesn't
keep the rain out, you know?

doesn't help the blind learn to walk or the lame to see, and
how many years did we spend wandering
lost down hospital hallways?

who exactly were we looking for?

the machines had been turned off,
the body forgotten

the sun was back, but without meaning

without warmth or color, and it was a
small apartment above a liquor store

it was a dying factory town on a polluted river
and we spent each day redefining the world

we talked about nothing,
        knew nothing,
and were we just the ghosts of our parents?

do we hate them
as much as they hated us?

and she stands naked in the silence of any
thursday afternoon and walks slowly to the window,
and you waste this one tiny portion of your life
writing everything down

you ask if she's happy
and she answers

says she needs to get back home
before her husband does and do you
remember how the doctor kept his eyes closed
while he explained the procedure?

forgetting is always an option,
                    i suppose

windows painted over and doors nailed shut and
the child was sick, yes,
but nothing was certain and
she asks *was it you?*

asks *did you make it?*

and he laughs, answers *yes* and then
answers *no,*
says *the child is gone,*
which is what i've been trying to explain

the shape of passing days

the deaths of every small moment

that last good summer,

but we didn't know it then
all of those hours we burned to
the ground thinking we were in love

a joke?

sure, but it's been a
long fucking time and i'm still
waiting for the punchline

3000 miles of silence and then a letter
from a shuttered room and
then nothing

and i'm not going to spend the
rest of my life saying good-bye

against empire

the poet and then
the poet dead and then just
one more person we forget and look –

you need to know how to
recognize the enemy

you need to stand in the shadows of starlings,
                            of crows,
and pretend to believe in
deeper meanings because
            seriously
how fucking hard is it to *not* start a war?

at what point do we decide we're
tired of letting our children
be slaughtered?

who will we sacrifice
in their place?

incantation for the refused

the rumor of your death or
the lie that is your life

        both
      maybe
and at the same time

sunlight and famine and
unpaid bills

the news of war
which is how we define both
the past and the future

a false king and a blind prophet
and the vast emptiness between them
where cities used to stand

have you forgotten how to cast a shadow?

are you a failed poet just
waiting for the moment when you
can become a forgotten suicide?

look

flags are for fools and
guns for cowards

refusal is the key

no masters
no slaves

nothing more holy than yourself

let the whores who would
buy and sell you
devour their own kind or
let them starve

let them be the corpses we
wrap in flags to burn
and then let them be nowhere,
                and then beyond

and sister lies, says she's
through digging graves

says the house was never a home
until it burned to the ground
but this isn't how i remember it

empty spaces
        yes

and the idea of escape,
but every door i opened only ever
led to rooms without doors

every junkie i fell in love with
was just looking for the
right moment to overdose

and sister laughs, tells me
self-hatred is a gift

tells me nothing that is lost
will ever return in
exactly the same form

but who among us sings and who forgets
the reasons why?

watches her lover
get into the burning car

another cold grey afternoon

another war, or maybe the same one
just moved to a different country

the fine art of killing some of
the children to save the others and
then the car drives off

screams?

no

smell of burning flesh, of gasoline,
and where am i when she calls?

where am i when
my mother finds my father on
the kitchen floor?

two questions without answers

the year of junkie suicides,
of no-talent overdoses

nine dollars an hour,
36 hours a week and everyone dies,
of course, but why am i just pretending
to be alive while i'm busy
doing it?

why does this girl with her
face painted white
want me to kiss her clean?

laughs when i ask her
her name

says her boyfriend won't be home for
another three hours at least,
usually stops to screw some married bitch
when he gets off work and she says
start with my feet

says *work your way up* and i can
still remember a time
when there was an art to bleeding

can still remember being
carsick in the back seat

being thrown into the deep end
and held under and
it's our fear that stays with us

it's her last lover
stepping into the bullet's path

fifty bucks from the cash register and
a twelve pack of schaeffer and
he's hit but never caught

and she marries a man who
never smiles, and she learns

hills and valleys

creeks and rivers

everything always in the process
of becoming something else

everyone alone

summer, which is where all of my
memories of you exist,
and then summer's end

burnt hill road on a sunday afternoon

dust-colored sky
just like all of my dreams

college education
and a dead-end job

a waitress i know gone in a car crash
down in north carolina

told me she loved me,
but she was drunk

broken arm which was a gift from
her boyfriend, and i was trying to remember
why i hadn't left this fucking town

i was living in a two-room apartment
down by the river,
pretending to be a painter

pretending to be a writer

pretending to be human, and i sucked at it
as bad as everyone i knew

sat on the floor in sammy's trailer
listening to the stones while some high school girl
he'd met at the gas station gave him head in
the bedroom

late winter, early spring, everything
without color and streaked with mud

a landscape defined by
abandoned warehouses and
burned-out gas stations and all of the
empty fields in between

a cop at the door wanting to
know what i knew, which was nothing

landlord with his gap-toothed smile,
his reek of pot and beer,
said there was a party upstairs

said his brother had been killed
in the war,
but he couldn't remember which one

said *dead is dead* and
walked down the hall and i am
tired of being whatever age i am

i am tired of no longer having
the strength to hate myself

last days of a desperate year,
children tear-gassed, poisoned, shot to

pieces by their own governments
fucked by men who claim to have
licked the ass of god and
tasted only honey and listen -

just shut the hell up and listen

you will answer the phone at
4:30 in the morning to receive the
news of your son's death
or this -

you will be six thousand miles away
on the day your
father is finally devoured by cancer

you won't have spoken to him for
almost fifteen years

it will take six weeks for
the news to find you

you'll laugh

will think about your own death,
but from a distance,
detached and unconvinced

these things happen, of course,
but almost always to someone else

almost always without reason

pretty goddamn funny

distant king

was holding the prayer in my
hands & was reminded of christ

was reminded of ernst

of dorothea

bitter smiles in an endless desert
and the way the hills looked
against the sky

believe it

no one had to force those
soldiers to kill the children

the idea of blood as an aphrodisiac
is nothing new

leave the bones out in the sunlight

water them

sing their tearstained praises

at some point you will
need to choose between buying
food or buying gas

at some point you will have to
give up your childish dreams
of fame and fortune

almost fifteen years now since
my father's death
and i still can't decide whether i
loved or hated him

i still can't stop looking
for a better option

and the grass is still green but
the back yard riddled with weeds
and august approaching

the ocean sleeping just beneath
the ground we walk upon

none of us remembered one
thousand years from now
which is probably the
most important thing

typhon's blues

brave men killing brave men until
it settles into a hypnotic rhythm

the dead and the dying and
whatever reasons they're given

two sisters hung from different branches
of the same tree just outside the
village they were born in and
                 of course
we're all guilty of something but
only those with power & wealth can turn
their denials into absolute truth

only those without use
human skulls to dig shallow graves

keep asking these whores you've elected
if we're at war and all they do is laugh

when everyone is the enemy
victory is no longer a possibility

a series of idle threats

three weeks of rain in the room of
murdered children and i don't doubt the
future for a second and i refuse to
believe in the past

salvation is the fist always
connecting with your face

the pills don't help but i still want more
and do you remember the dream?

snow in august and all of the strangers
who smiled as the noose was tied
around your neck

fat man in an anonymous cubicle
pointing to the numbers on
his computer screen, keeps telling me
how much he matters, how much he's worth
but i'm up too high to care

pure sunlight shot into my veins

the sound of angels fucking

beyond holy and without borders and
do you remember how much you

hated your father and how
much of a disappointment you were to him?

none of us deserves hope but
sometimes it's all we can score

sometimes it's the episode where
god was the devil

where he was twin twelve year-old girls
and sometimes i weep for the
future that will never arrive

the age of reason gives way
to the age of brute force

entire villages are slaughtered to
make some vague irrelevant point about
some vague irrelevant prophet and
do you remember how good it felt licking
the salt from each other's wounds?

tasted like fear and like subtle
desperation and it was always cold
in the house

were always ghosts in every room

cobain with a needle in his arm and
whining about the pain and
the days negated

all warmth nullified

asshole always had a smile on his
face while he denied his addictions and
we let him and were you there
when the body of the minister's wife was
found in the dumpster behind
the truck stop?

did you get stoned with
the dishwasher after work?

screw his sister and then shoot out
the headlights on her boyfriend's car?

and what about your marriage and
what about your divorce?

do you have any memories at all of
the only woman you ever really loved?

how you cut the soles of her feet
wide open with a razor blade then made
her walk three miles home through
the freezing rain?

i have never doubted that fear is
the most holy of weapons

mantra for beaten dogs

and this isn't the news of yr
mother's death, but
maybe just an early rumor

last days of winter or the
first of spring,
frozen clouds in a blue sky, the
inevitability of another new war
in another doomed country

couldn't feel my hands as i
reached into the river, but
i knew they were there

knew the children would be
crying when i found them, knew
they'd want reassuring lies, and
if i stared hard enough at the sun
i could almost make myself
believe in a better future

if i sat perfectly still in my
father's house, i could still hear
him tell me what a
disappointment i was

can feel what little warmth is
left in this day fade with
the light

will laugh at the thought of
outliving every motherfucker
who ever tried to fill my
heart with fear

final poem from a blue notebook

in motion & sunlight with the
shadows of clouds with the
    kiss of judas

    no hope but
     strength

no distance greater than the
one we've put between us

and this is where the forest ends and
this is where the desert begins

this is diane in her sudden old age

frightened but not angry and
if there is comfort to be found in the
world of words & actions it's the
    comfort of despair

it's the bleak joy of futility

we fuck to make ourselves numb

i dream in shades of
green and grey

spend afternoons lost in neighborhoods
where nothing moves where
no one speaks and the
houses there repeating themselves
                          endlessly

the smell of gasoline
or of burning plastic

the news of christ's arrival
and then his crucifixion

a fist in the face of
a newborn child

a boot heel down squarely on
its skull and there is only the world you
inherit or the one you create

there is only this one twisted gift
this ability to create hatred from nothing
and what i regret most in my life
is losing beth

thirty years of empty gestures and
wasted days and it was
always the wrong country

i had always brought
the wrong map

was lost in this town that i only
ever wanted to leave and
if i believed in anything
it was the power of inertia

if i wasn't such a gutless coward
i'd consider suicide
        but not now

not early evening at the end of
july, flowers vines crawling up the
sides of the house, my children
laughing, because faith is a
gift that fades

not everyone is blessed

drive to work in the morning or
to the store at night,
windows down,
spirit of eden on the cd player and
the streets everywhere lined with
the unwanted and the forgotten,
the starving, the raped, the
endlessly broken and do you
feel guilty saving just yourself?

are your memories worth
the pain they bring?

listen

the people in power will always
tell you what they think
you should believe
and they always devour whoever it is
you hold most dear

they will offer you small
amounts of freedom but only
for a price

the price will always be
more than you can afford

just kill the driver while you can and
run from the car towards
the hopeless warmth of the sun

speech in the ruins of what was given to me

and who will cut out the
throats of the jackal-headed priests and
who will set fire to the corpses of
these demagogues and self-proclaimed kings?

who will plant the seeds of the future
in their smouldering ashes?

this might finally be
someone worth listening to

traitor

this jackal-headed whore
with my words
falling out of his mouth

with my splintered teeth
held in his claws and
my puke staining his shoes and
does he think any of this
shit is easy?

does he understand the
pain that comes with bleeding?

what i need is
to be farther away

what i need is to take aim

just bang-bang and
fuck you and goodbye

John Sweet (b. 1968) is a believer in writing as catharsis, and in emotional synesthesia. He has been publishing in the small press for 30 years. Among his collections are *Human Cathedrals* (Ravenna Press), *Bastard Faith* (Scars Publications), a series of acclaimed limited-edition chapbooks from Kendra Steiner Editions, and *The Century Of Dreaming Monsters* (winner of the 2014 Lummox Poetry Prize). He lives in upstate New York.